Peppa Pig's Family Computer

Mummy Pig is working on the family computer. She is typing very fast. Mummy Pig has a lot of important work to do today.

Daddy Pig is in the kitchen making soup for lunch.

"Daddy?" Peppa asks. "Can we go and watch Mummy on the computer, please?"
"Yes, as long as you don't disturb her," Daddy Pig says.

"Mummy?" Peppa asks. "Can George and I sit on your lap and watch you work?"

"Yes, as long as you both sit quietly,"
Mummy Pig agrees.

About a minute later, Peppa asks, "Can we play the Happy Mrs Chicken game on the computer?"

Mummy Pig says, "We can play Happy Mrs Chicken later. But now I have to work."

Another minute later, Peppa asks, "Mummy? Can we help you work?" Peppa taps away at the computer like Mummy Pig.

"Yes, George," Peppa says in a bossy voice.
"You mustn't do this." Peppa taps away again
and the computer flashes.

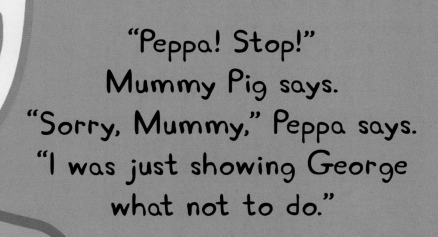

"Peppa! Stop!"
Mummy Pig says.
"Sorry, Mummy," Peppa says.
"I was just showing George
what not to do."

"Daddy Pig!" Mummy calls. "Can you mend the computer while I finish the lunch?"
"Uh . . ." Daddy Pig says. "I'm not very good with these things."

"Hmmm . . ." Daddy Pig pushes a button.

"Mmmm . . ." Daddy Pig pushes another button.

"Maybe if I switch it off and switch it on again . . ."

Daddy Pig has mended the computer!
"Hooray, Daddy!" shouts Peppa.

She and George jump up and down.
"Yes," Daddy Pig smiles. "I am a bit of
an expert at these things."

"Daddy," Peppa asks. "Can we play that computer game, Happy Mrs Chicken? Mummy said we could play it later," Peppa says. "And now it's later!"

"Well," Daddy Pig thinks for a moment,
"OK then." Daddy Pig starts
the Happy Mrs Chicken game.

"Ho, ho, ho!" Daddy Pig laughs as Peppa
and George play Happy Mrs Chicken.
"Snort!" Mummy Pig says as she comes into the room.
"I see the computer is working again!"